Contents

Small Talk...

The Power of Small Talk

The Power of Small Talk a Business Environment

The Power of Small Talk in Relationships and Social Situations

Getting Over Your Fear

Social Anxiety

How to Start a Conversation

Where to Practice

Making an Awesome Impression

The Keys to an Awesome First Impression

Being Approachable

How to Not Look Like a Creep or Pick Up Artist

Physical Appearance

What to Say (and Not to Say)

Keep the Conversation Going

It Takes Two to Tango

Smoothly Ending a Conversation

Closing Thoughts

Small Talk...

Small talk... it's something you have to do on a daily basis, yet it never seems to get any easier.

You're probably normally perfectly confident, but the second it comes to making small talk you have no idea what to say, you freeze up, embarrass yourself, and leave the situation feel down and dejected.

Small talk doesn't have to be like this though; it can be fun, exciting, and incredibly useful for improving your life. However, most of us never get to experience this; most of us never reap the incredible benefits of small talk as we don't have the necessary skills to harness it.

If you're anything like I used to be, then you will know the awful feeling that comes with bumbling your way through a conversation.

I used to shy away from small talk as I would start to sweat, feel nervous, say ridiculous things, and make conversational faux-pas that would leave an awkward silence hanging in the air. One of those silences that seems to last forever and has people awkwardly shuffling on their feet avoiding eye contact.

After one too many of those situations, I found it was simply easier to not even attempt to make small talk. I found it much less painless to just avoid conversations and keep to myself. I thought this was great for a while, but it soon started to affect my relationship and my work – and not in a good way.

My work stopped respecting me as they couldn't rely on me to close deals, network, or generally just be a part of the office community. My girlfriend also got sick of taking me to parties or events, which almost tore us apart.

It took me a long time to take action against the negativity in my life, but I did take action, and now I've been able to reverse the effects of those darker times. I want to show you how I did it so that if you're in a similar situation, you can take back control of your life.

You might be like I was, perfectly confident in comfortable, familiar environments, but the moment you have to make small talk you become a different person - a pathetic version of yourself that you hate.

If you've ever been in the situation where you hate yourself for not being able to make small talk, then this book is your cure.

This book is going to teach you exactly how to master small talk so that you can effortlessly converse with anyone. No matter what the environment is you will be able to chat to people in a way that not only makes them like you, but can massively improve your life.

You might not know it, but understanding and mastering small talk is one of the fastest ways to improve your life. Want to meet a new partner? Want to explore new business ventures? Want to climb the corporate ladder? Want to avoid being laid off? Or maybe you just want to pass a boring plane journey?

Whatever your goals are, the skill of making effortless small talk is absolutely essential.

I won't be teaching you to rhyme off random, memorized lines. No, this book is about learning to make natural small talk that draws people towards you, makes them like you, and has you actually enjoy making small talk.

You will be learning everything from the power of small talk and how to leverage it for success; all the way to decoding the body language of others and making a winning first impression.

So, if you've ever wanted to learn the art of small talk, conquer your fears, and have the ability to talk to anyone, anywhere, at any time then you're going to love this book.

Effortless Small Talk is the easiest to adopt approach to mastering small talk that is available. I don't teach you hundreds of strategies that contradict each other and take months to learn, instead I provide you with the simplest and most effective strategies and provide them with step-by-step instructions so that you can implement them today.

I'm looking forward to going on this journey with you and helping you become the best version of yourself, so let's get started.

The Power of Small Talk

Most people view small talk with a degree of disdain and believe it is good for only two things: killing time whilst waiting, and having something to do at parties. Otherwise, it's a nuisance at best and torture at worst.

After all, once the conversational taboos of politics, religion, and sex are crossed off the small talk list, there just isn't that much to talk about, aside from current events, weather, sports, and the latest entertainment offerings.

It doesn't help that the name for this activity, "small talk," implies mindless blather about nothing of significance. I mean, let's face it small talk, isn't going to have you delve into the philosophy of Aristotle (unless you're at a philosophers' convention), but something nearly everyone forgets is - small talk doesn't have to be on topics of no value. Once you grasp this concept and get over your misconceptions of it, you see that small talk has real power.

Just as animals use their sense of smell to learn about each other and use their behaviors to express the social pecking order, humans use language to do the same thing (we also use our behaviors to establish the social pecking order, but that's a discussion for a later chapter). When you're talking to another person, you're gathering information about them. For instance, you discover their values, their social status, commonalities you share with them, and much more. We do this as it has been shown that humans like to associate with people similar to themselves. A phenomenon social scientists call *homophily*, and what better way to find people similar to you than to talk to them?

This, in essence, is the power and importance of small talk.

Finding out more about someone, through small talk, allows you to form new relationships, build friendships, explore business opportunities, and open up your world to a whole host of situations that would have previously remained hidden.

The Power of Small Talk a Business Environment

The business world is all about power: who has it, and who doesn't.

Most companies have clear rules – both written and unwritten – about what information can be shared between which people, and the channels through which it can be shared. Much of this is, of course, to prevent leaks, maintain competitive advantages, and keep the lawyers and regulators happy. But some of this is to maintain the power structure and pecking order. These rules must be followed in the workplace because there are consequences to one's career when they aren't, but small talk can help you skirt these rules to accelerate your success.

Properly done, small talk will be informal and relaxed; it will encourage open discussions and the sharing of information between people who may never have socially conversed previously. For example; the manager who gave you a wilting look for asking an inappropriate question during a meeting may be telling you all about his recent fishing trip at an after-work pub visit. Given that you work together, eventually and inevitably, the conversation will move to 'talking shop.' During this conversation you will, not only gather information that may be useful in getting a promotion or surviving a layoff, but you will also develop a relationship with the people above you. This is of crucial importance as it has been shown time and time again, that those who have closer relationships with their superiors are not only paid higher, but also survive layoffs and are more likely to be picked for promotions.

This of course isn't fair, but it's how the world works and knowing it will benefit you immensely.

In addition to career guidance and progression, small talk benefits your creativity as it gives you the opportunity to exchange ideas and solve problems with others. A pop-culture example of this would be from the film, 'Thank You for Smoking.' Nick Naylor, the PR chief for the tobacco lobby, meets with those who work for the alcohol and firearms lobbies. Over lunch and cocktails, they talk about challenges they face as public spokespeople for unpopular industries. They discuss what works and what strategies to avoid. They each find strength in the group, and at the end of the movie, the three are joined by others seeking the same professional support. In a real-life business environment this is often exactly how small talk can play out and you will find that conversing with those in similar situations to you will open new avenues, reveal previously unidentified solutions, and allow you to form cross-industry relationships that add incredible value.

Small talk can also be harnessed to reframe your existing workplace relationships by removing people from their pedestals and leveling out the structure of seniority. Many people are intimidated by senior management, especially if they are several levels below them on the corporate food chain. However, by making small talk with these managers, you will find that they are people just like you. And, as you explore it further you will find out that you have more in common with them than you could have previously imagined. No longer will you just be someone the boss nods and smiles to in the hallway, you will be their friend – it may only be on a work-friendship basis, but the power of this is massive.

If right now you're wondering, "Why would my boss want to talk to me?" Well, remember that most people like to chat with new people and are grateful to converse with someone who is outside their immediate circle. People tire of the same daily conversations, with the same people. And this is especially true in the close-knit groups that exist within upper management chains.

An incredibly powerful result that springs from your new relationship with your boss is that people will start to seek you out as they see you as someone who has the inside scoop. And even if you don't have the inside scoop, people will perceive that you do - you will soon become the person to know, and in a world where information is power, that is a very enviable position to be in.

The Power of Small Talk in Relationships and Social Situations

Small talk is an essential tool for maintaining out-of-work relationships. Not only does it help to resolve anxiety and promote relaxation, it allows the personal bonds we've built over time to be maintained and improved.

The importance of being able to properly make small-talk can easily be understood when you study romantic relationships. In the initial several months, or years, the new couple has endless things to talk about. They are discovering each other and the conversation will always flow. However, as time progresses, couples will often find that conversations can begin to lag. This has nothing to do with how they feel towards each other or that the relationship is failing, it is simply the natural progression that happens when two people have spent an extended amount of time together. If you want to see an example of this just look around you the next time you're at a restaurant. I can guarantee you will see couples sitting in silence.

Now, those people who have not mastered the art of effortless small-talk will often find these situations difficult, but if you know how to spark the conversation, you will find that these situations simple do not exist as you can naturally initiate small talk – which, as previously mentioned, leads into a flowing, natural conversation.

Small talk can be used at times where there is natural anxiety to ease tensions and distract people from their stress. Two perfect examples of this are hospitals and airports.
 Oftentimes people who are in an emotionally tense situation are looking for a distraction to help them cope; by conversing with them you not only pass your time but you help someone who is in a difficult place – and who knows, you may even make a new friend.

Getting Over Your Fear

It's the night of your spouse's best-friends party. You've checked yourself in the mirror. You're looking great. Your hair looks awesome and you're ready to rock and roll, but as you're standing in front of the door waiting for the hostess to let you in… anxiety hits. You go from your normally confident self to a quivering, blushing mess. As you enter the room, your pulse is racing, your mouth dries out, you feel yourself sweat a little, and now that secluded chair in the corner of the room is calling you. But you know you can't go to it. So, you settle in for a drink and awkwardly stand next to your partner the whole evening, stumbling through conversations, before finding an excuse to leave early.

Have you ever been in a similar situation to that one?

As you picked up this book I'm going to guess that you have… maybe too many times.

Anxiety in social situations is normal for the vast majority of people (some just hide it well), and this is especially true if it involves meeting new people or being in an unfamiliar setting.

You may find, for example, that you can talk freely with co-workers at the office, but you would sooner gnaw off your own arm before socializing with them at an awards banquet. The people are the same; it's the context that's different.

You may simply prefer the company of small groups of close friends or staying in alone to read a good book than going to a party, and that's okay. Not everyone is the life of the party, and not everyone *wants* to be the life of the party. However, the time will come when you're obligated to go to a social gathering - one where you will be expected to make small talk, and even if you don't want to go, you know you have to.

It's when these situations occur that knowing how to effortless make small talk will be an immeasurable asset to you.

So, let's dive into it…

Social Anxiety

Firstly to understand why some people can't make small talk effectively, we need to study the area of social anxiety. Social anxiety nearly always stems from one's fear of being judged and rejected.

But why do we fear this judgment and rejection?

Well, every social interaction involves judging others and being judged, and when we don't pass other's expectations it hurts. Some people accept that rejection is a possibility and take it in their stride when it happens. Some people, however, get upset, take it to heart and start to avoid situations where they fear that they may face rejection.

Most of the time, it's simple avoidance – they don't want to be hurt, so they learn to avoid the source of the pain. In the extreme though, social anxiety can cause significant impairment and damage to one's life, especially if you avoid situations where you are expected to be present, such as those for work or for family. Certain people can even suffer severe physical symptoms just by thinking about the prospect of social situations they are expected to attend.

For the purposes of this book we will assume that your anxiety is mild, and that you just need some strategies and tips to implement so you can get over your social anxiety, make an incredible first impression and learn to make small-talk so you can improve all areas of your life.

If wild horses couldn't drag you into a social gathering, or if your anxiety severely impacts your life, then please see your doctor. He can offer medication and counseling to help you.

How to Start a Conversation

Walking into the room is only part of the battle. Finding someone to talk to is another part. (The third part is finding something to talk about and that'll be covered later.)

When you're in a situation where small talk is essential, the first thing to pay attention to is body language. Since most people show approachability through their body language, it's usually not difficult to tell whether someone would prefer to be approached or left alone. For example, someone reading a book on the bus is probably going to want to be left alone, but someone looking out the window or just sitting there quietly making eye contact may welcome conversation.

But how do you start one?

Many people are afraid to initiate conversation because they don't want to be embarrassed, it comes back to the social anxiety we discussed earlier – they fear being judged and rejected. People don't want to say something offensive or make the other person uncomfortable, so they "play it safe" and don't say anything. This is not a healthy approach; the "play it safe" method is simply an excuse to not overcome the fear of making small talk. Not crushing this fear means they miss out on some great opportunities to meet other people, form new relationships and improve their life in a number of ways.

This book is going to make sure you never need to be this person who hides behind the "play it safe" excuse.

One of the most effective ways to start a conversation is to use Dr. Carol Fleming's three-step method called 'ARE' - Anchor, Reveal, Encourage.

This method starts a conversation with a general, superficial statement. Which seamlessly transitions into the more specific, then into comments and questions which draw the other person out of their shell and encourages them to naturally keep the conversation going.

The first step, Anchor, simply has you make a statement based on some common experience. For example, at a business luncheon, you might comment on the weather, the food, the speaker, or some other aspect of the event that you can both relate to. You might say, *"I'm so glad we were able to get Dr. Parker to speak today."* Because the other person (or people, since this technique works with groups) understands what you are talking about, you've got a framework on which to build a conversation.

One key point to note here is, many people fear the initial opening of a conversation as they feel the need to say something interesting, clever or witty. This, in actuality, is not at all important and is not recommended. Not only does it make the idea of small talk seem tougher, but you also run the risk of offending them as you don't know the other persons humor, tastes or personality.

Instead, focus upon initiating the conversation with a simple statement that has a shared commonality.

The second step, Reveal, has you make a more personal statement about the Anchor. The Anchor, in other words, is the door you've opened, and the Reveal allows you and the other person to walk through it together. If you're talking about the keynote speaker, you may tack on *"I read his book about marketing, and it was brilliant, I absolutely loved it!"* This allows for more common ground because you've given personal information about yourself, and you've extended an invitation for the other person to join in, ask questions and offer their own 2 cents.

The third step, Encourage, has you asking a question related to the Anchor and the Reveal. You might ask the other person how they're familiar with Dr. Parker, or if they've read the book, or something similar. Once you've gotten to the

Encourage stage, it's important to use guiding questions and comments to keep the small talk flowing. A guiding question is intended to get a response other than a simple "yes" or "no." Your goal is to encourage them to open up and talk, not to cross-examine them.

A guiding question might have you ask something like, *"What got you interested in the entrepreneurship?"* Or, *"I'd love to hear more about your experiences in entrepreneurship, what sort of areas have you explored before?"* These simple sentences will keep the conversation from fading into awkward silences and as you're guiding the other person along it guarantees that you won't run out of things to talk about.

So to get started with the Anchor from ARE – you need an opening comment. If you can't think of any off the bat here are some common 'openers,' you might want to use in various situations I've listed a few of my favorites before. These are all tried and tested, some may seem overly simple but remember the 'A' from ARE – it's just about getting the conversation started.

For literally any situation:
"Hey, how are you?"

In a coffee shop:
"Sorry, I was just wondering… is a 'Grande' the equivalent of a large or medium?"

As you walk from outside to an indoor location:

"Wow, it's horrible/lovely out there!"

Waiting in any shop queue:

"Does this shop/place always have such long lines?"

If someone is holding a book or has it sitting next to them:

"Sorry to disturb you… but how are you finding [book title] I've been considering reading it?"

To someone walking their dog:

"Wow, aren't you a cute thing? (talk initially to the dog, then say to the owner) Your dog is gorgeous, what breed is she/he?

Where to Practice

The ARE method is excellent, and it's easy to learn, but like any other skill, it takes practice. Fortunately, there are almost unlimited places to practice and I have a step-by-step approach to conquering your fears and insecurities so that you can master small talk.

The best way to master small talk is to start with people you already know, acquaintances and co-workers are usually the best options. They already know you and that tends to lower the risk and, therefore, your stress levels. By doing this, it will allow you to practice the ARE steps in a non-threatening environment where the stakes are low.

After this, I suggest practicing in situations where you are unlikely to ever encounter the other person again, or in situations that don't really matter. Start small; make a passing comment to someone whilst waiting in line at Starbucks or whilst waiting on a train. Doing this clears the hurdle of talking to a complete stranger. Don't aim to engage them in small-talk, just make a simple passing comment. If you start to feel nervous about this then repeat the following to yourself (in your head, not out loud):

"I'm never going to see this person again. I have nothing to lose and everything to gain. My fear is completely irrational and I won't be held back by it any longer!"

Once you're over the hurdle of saying a single comment to a stranger, it is time to engage a stranger in small talk.

For this step you ideally want to use what's called a 'warm open.' This is simply when you leverage a mutual connection to introduce you to a stranger. Due to your mutual connection you are both already "pre-sold" on the other person – the mutual connection ensures the other person already knows that you're a good, safe person and therefore engaging in small talk is much easier.

A good place to practice this is at a gathering where you don't really know anyone, especially when it's a group in which you don't have a lot invested. Ask the host to introduce you to another guest and practice these skills on that person. You may hit it off and become fast, lifelong friends, or you may never see this person again. Either way, you've found an opportunity to practice your new small talk skills.

As any musician or actor knows, the more you rehearse, the better you perform. Take every possible opportunity to engage in small talk, no matter where or with whom. You'll be surprised at how quickly your skills develop.

Making an Awesome Impression

Everyone knows this guy. He's the one who oozes into the room, sidles up to the most attractive woman, and tries to chat her up, even when she's clearly not interested. His idea of small talk falls into three general categories: sexual innuendoes, off-color jokes, and political commentary, and he tries to rationalize his offensive behavior with a nudge in the ribs (sometimes literally) and a, "You know I'm just jokin', right?"

This is a memorable first impression, and it shows a certain amount of confidence, but that's not a good impression. In fact, it's actually a very poor impression because it's memorable for the wrong reasons. He doesn't respect personal boundaries – physical or social – and what's worse, doesn't *care*. You remember him because he made you feel uncomfortable and that's not a good thing.

Whether you like it or not, or whether you think it's fair or not, first impressions are about judging others and being judged ourselves. Good impressions are about making other people like us enough to want to include us in their group. When it comes down to it, first impressions matter a lot. Do not underestimate the power of them.

And one of the keys to being able to make effortless small talk is to make a good first impression – doing this means people feel comfortable talking with you, want to meet you, and will warm to you very quickly.

The Keys to an Awesome First Impression

When meeting people for the first time, the best impression you can make is to appear relaxed, confident, and ready to engage other people. You want to be someone that others want to connect with. This is generally easier said than done, especially when you're nervous, but there are some simple strategies to accomplish this.

When you meet someone for the first time, they judge you on what they see because they have nothing else to go on.

So when they see someone who can't or won't make eye contact, who appears fidgety, who doesn't smile, and who doesn't look like they want to be there, they'll dismiss you without a second thought. Many of these behaviors are culturally transmitted, meaning the other person is probably not aware that they are judging you, but they are nonetheless so don't think you can skip this step.

We are going to be covering strategies for making eye contact, genuinely smiling, promoting the correct body language, and a few simple mind hacks you can use to open the small-talk door by always making a great first impression.

If you have difficulty making eye contact, try lightly focusing on the person's ear, or to a point just behind their head. This will make you appear to looking them in the eye, but you're really not. It's just a way to trick your brain into doing something it's not comfortable doing. If you feel confident enough to directly look into someone's eyes then make sure you follow these steps to not appear too intense or creepy:

> Look into their eyes but don't stare. Blink naturally.

> Make natural breaks in the eye contact. Don't continually look into their eyes.

Break contact roughly every three-four seconds by glancing away.

Fidgeting is a sign of nervousness, not only does it reduce your appearance of confidence, but it also makes others uncomfortable. A simple way to avoid fidgeting is to find something to hold that's appropriate to the situation. If there is nothing to hold then just lightly clasp your hands in a relaxed grip – a tight grip promotes nervousness, and others will subconsciously pick up on this.

Smiling and relaxing are tougher to do convincingly because you look like a fake if it doesn't seem natural. Giving someone a fleeting two-second smile, then going back to a straight face is telling them that you'd rather count the dimples on a golf ball than talk to them. And if you're not relaxed, you'll look nervous and uncomfortable.

The key to being able to smile naturally is to enter a relaxed, positive state just before the event. Try listening to your favorite music or a comedy album on the way to the event. It's hard not to relax when you're listening to your favorite musician or comedian, and that elevated emotional state will continue when you get to the event. Once you're at the event, another simple strategy is to replay the memories of funny or happy events from your life. Triggering these memories will result in your brain associating those feelings with your current situation. Harness these memories and before you know it you will be smiling naturally without consciously knowing it.

Another powerful psychological hack for "saying" the right things with your body language and imbuing yourself with confidence is to practice power posing. Popularized by Amy Cuddy in her famous TED Talk, power posing is a simple 1-2 minute exercise that has incredible results on your confidence, happiness, and even cognitive functioning. I highly recommend that you check out her TED Talk, but if you don't have time here is a quick primer on how to power pose.

Before an event that you're feeling nervous about, simply go somewhere quiet (like a bathroom stall) then strike and hold a power pose. A power pose is any standing position that represents a powerful stance, a classic example is the superhero pose – hands on your hips, chest out, head help high and a feeling of dominance. This may sound ridiculous, but the research behind it is outstanding. Try it just once, it only takes 1-2 minutes, and you will feel the difference instantly.

The physical space you occupy also plays a role in the impression you signal to people. You're going to want to pay particular attention to personal space and touching. In a business setting, most people are fine with a handshake and not much more than that. For standing distance, one arm's length is generally considered the boundary here. It's close enough that you can hear, but not so close that you're making the other person feel crowded.

In a more informal setting, its okay to move a bit closer, but let the other person set the distance. If you're touchy-feely, you definitely want to tone it down, and if you have issues with people touching you, remember that you will be sending nonverbal messages about that – so take note as it will impact your approachability.

Finally, take note that the best impression you can make is to be yourself.

People like and respect genuineness, and they especially respect sincerity. If you try to shy away from who you naturally are - hiding your passions and your personality - people will feel something is "off" about you. They may not be able to place their finger on exactly what it is, but there will be a feeling "they just can't quite describe." I'm sure you've personally experienced this before when meeting new people.

So, own who you are, be proud of it and be genuine, if you do this then conversations with flow with ease, people will warm to you and people will find you very approachable.

On the topic of people approaching you there is a few points I would like to mention to increase your approachability.

Being Approachable

You don't always have to be the one to initiate conversation. Other people may want to get to know *you*. In order for this to happen, you have to be approachable.

Being approachable involves more than just standing there looking available. It's about sending the right signals so that other people know you want to talk. For example, standing away from the main group with your arms crossed is a good way to keep people away, because with this body language you're basically telling them to stay away and leave you alone. On the other hand, leaning into the group, with your body open, and making eye contact tells them you want to be involved and you want to talk.

A closed off person is easily represented by the way they hold themselves. You will notice that they are always bundled up in their own safe zone – arms crossed, head down, no smile. If you want people to approach you, don't be this person, instead look around the room, make eye contact, follow it up with a brief 1 second smile, and stand with a casual pose to give the appearance of openness.

How to Not Look Like a Creep or Pick Up Artist

Looking like a creep defeats the entire purpose of learning how to make small talk. You can memorize an entire dictionary of small talk topics, but if you can't (or won't) control your behavior toward the other person, then all of the preparation in the world will not help you.

This is something most coaches won't tell you, instead of focusing on how to make engaging and entertaining small talk they simply have you rhyme off different situational based 'openers.' If you've ever been in a conversation with someone "reading from a playbook" you will know how unnatural it feels.

The single best way to prevent creepiness is to keep a close mind to your body language. Continually staring at another person before approaching them, not making eye contact (or making too much eye contact), and invading private spaces are all very off-putting and make people feel uneasy around you.

Along with body language goes overall demeanor. It's one thing to want to talk to someone for a while. It's another to follow this person around for the duration of the event. Additionally remember that no-one likes a wet blanket. So, unloading all of your problems on the other person is a surefire way to make them distance themselves from you, as is only talking about your favorite topic. Interesting small talk changes subjects from time to time, so if you're a one-trick pony, it's time to learn some new ones.

It's also important to respect other people's physical and emotional boundaries. Although asking about family is ordinarily a good topic for small talk, remember that someone may be going through a difficult time with theirs and may not want to talk about it. Although you think you are being supportive by encouraging the other person to open up, he/she may think you are being presumptuous and keep their distance from you.

Jokes at the other person's expense also fall into this category because until you really get to know someone, you don't always know what their triggers are. A simple, well-intentioned joke may be enough to upset them – you may remember that this was mentioned earlier in regards to opening a conversation.

Finally, if you don't want to look like a pickup artist, don't use pickup lines. If you want to get the attention of someone you're attracted to, there is no better way to do this than to be genuine. Unless you can play off a pickup line for laughs (and not many can), just make small talk to kick-start the conversation then let it naturally flow into a real, meaningful conversation.

Physical Appearance

The old adage, "don't judge a book by its cover," doesn't apply to human relationships. It may seem unfair that others judge us by what they see, but that is all they initially have. When you are meeting people for the first time, make sure you dress appropriately for the occasion. If it's a business get-together, find out if the dress code is a suit and tie, business casual, or something else, and no matter what the dress code, make sure your clothes are clean, well-fitting, in good repair, and in a current style. Unless you're going to a disco convention, a plaid suit, open shirt, and heavy gold chain is going to make you stand out, and not in a good way.

What to Say (and Not to Say)

What *Not* to Talk About

Because the list of conversational topics available is limited only by your imagination and curiosity, it makes more sense to firstly list the topics that are, for most circumstances, off limits. These topics tend to make people feel uncomfortable at best and are often very offensive at their worst. As the goal of small talk is to make people feel comfortable around you, it doesn't make a lot of sense to alienate them, so what should you avoid?

Although any topic, no matter how innocent the intention, has the potential to cause offense. Multiple social studies have shown that some are almost guaranteed to cause problems. They are, of course, the Big Three: sex, religion, and politics. These are generally not appropriate in most circumstances, although if you are at, say, a church retreat or a meeting of your local political party, religion and politics are going to be the main topics of conversation. Other topics to avoid early on in the conversation are money, relationships, health problems and family issues. Each of these, however, will often naturally rise up during the meandering nature of the conversation, and if they do then feel free to explore them – just be sure to tread carefully.

The best guideline I can offer is to use your own judgement and read the other person's responses.

What to Talk About

So now that you know what *not* to talk about, it's time to find topics you *can* talk about. As I mentioned, the list is limited only by your curiosity and your imagination, but there are some old favorites.

Most people love to talk about themselves, so you might ask about where they've lived, what they do for a living, their hobbies, where they've traveled, and anything else within the bounds of good taste. It always pays to be observant; the guy wearing the Iron Man necktie is probably going to be a comic book fan and will be wearing that tie to let everyone know he is a fan.

Another good topic is popular culture. Just about everyone enjoys music, movies, books, and television, and most people will share their favorites with you, and you can share your favorites with them. It's perfectly all right if you have nothing in common because a mutual hatred for the same things can often be more fun than talking about things you both like.

Food is another strong small talk topic. Not everyone drinks, but everyone eats and everyone has a favorite food. Ask about their favorite cuisine. Is it Chinese, Japanese, French, Ghanaian, or Mexican? Can they recommend a good restaurant? Do they like to cook, and if they do, what do they like to cook? (Who knows? You may even be invited for dinner some night!) What are their favorite snacks, comfort foods, ice cream flavors? If money and calories was no object, what would they eat? If they could only eat one food for the rest of their life what would it be?

Ask about travel. Do they have plans for summer? Have they been anywhere exotic? Where is their favorite place to go on vacation? Where would they like to go? What is their favorite city? What is it you love about that city? If they could live anywhere, where would they live, and why?

Work is sometimes a safe topic. Where do they work? What do they do? How did they decide on that career? Do they have any great work stories they can tell?

If they're unemployed, or you are, don't be afraid to make or ask for referrals for jobs. If you know of something, sharing would be appreciated, and if you need something, the other person may be able to help.

Compliments work well, if there is something to compliment. If the person is wearing an interesting T-shirt, a goofy tie, is carrying a book you've read, or something else you like, it's okay to pay a compliment about it, or at least ask about it. "That's a cool tote bag." "What's your favorite NPR show?" Mine's . . . *Wait, Wait Don't Tell Me.*"

And don't forget what brought you together. How do they know the host? How did they get involved in the organization? Why is this cause interesting to them? Have they been involved for a long time? Do you know anyone else in common through the organization?

Keep the Conversation Going

So you've got a structure to work from and it's going great, but what do when you run out of things to talk about?

Relax. That probably won't happen. Good small talk takes a topic, builds on it, and takes it in different directions until it's time to move on to the next topic. For there to be good small talk you have to know how to ask open-ended questions based on what the other person is saying, and the way to do that is by paying attention.

Knowing what questions to ask is a bit of an art and will take practice but in general, you want to stay away from any question that can be answered with a simple "yes" or "no" answer. For instance, if you ask, "Did you like the speaker?" You're giving the other person the option to give a yes or no answer. However if you had phrased it, "What did you think about the speaker?" You are inviting them to provide feedback and answer with more than a curt yes or no. Using this strategy also means that in their answer they will provide multiple other avenues for you to pursue.

Now that you know to ask open-ended questions I want to describe another excellent strategy you should add to your repertoire. This strategy is incredibly powerful and research has shown it will increase a stranger's response to you, make them want to continue conversing with you and best of all, it allows you to speak less while appearing more likable. What is the strategy then?

The 2:1 Ratio.

Simply put, the other person should be talking twice as much as you. This all comes down to the fact that people love to talk about themselves, most people prefer talking over listening and ever speaker wants an attentive audience.

The key to the 2:1 Ratio is asking open-ended and follow-up questions, which you now know how to do. The ratio doesn't mean you must ensure you speak exactly half the time they do, instead it means that you should simply be aware that you should be speaking less than the other participants. During the back-and-forth of the conversation don't purposefully keep your answers short, just be careful not to drone on for 3 minutes – if you do you will see their attention wander. Instead answer their question then flip the conversation back to them with a simple phrase such as: "What are your thoughts on that?" or "Do you agree or do you have a different opinion?"

The 2:1 Ratio is an excellent technique for reducing your involvement in the conversation while making the other person more drawn to you, which is not an easy thing to do – and that is the power of the 2:1 Ratio.

It Takes Two to Tango

Thus far, the focus has been on you. You've learned how to get over social anxiety, how to start a conversation, how to find practice partners, how to make a good impression, and the social acceptable topics of conversations. But just as it takes two to tango, and it takes two (or more) to engage in small talk.

Open-ended questions allow the other person to share more about themselves, but you have to give them the opportunity to answer you. The key here is simply to listen and not talk over someone or interrupt them.

It's one thing to talk over someone because you're nervous, but to do so consistently implies to the other person that you're really not interested in anything they have to say. So, when you ask a question, leave a beat or two for the other person to answer, and then really listen to what they say. By being an attentive audience you are being respectful to the other person whilst gaining all the information you need to structure your next question.

We now need to cover the last component of small talk. Silence.

Silence happens, and when it does, let it. Don't be afraid of it.

However, if you're looking to keep the conversation going then there is a simple trick you can use to spark it back up and kill any silence…

Simply invite someone else into the conversation.

There are two main ways you can do this.

- You can signal someone to come over and then initiate them into the conversation by saying something along the lines of, "I was telling Josh here about how our company did XYZ, and I know you were integral to the success of the project –so I thought you might be able to explain it better than me…"

Or;

- You can say to the person you're speaking with something along the lines of, "I know who would have some awesome insights into this topic, Tony, fancy going to find him with me and pick his brain?"

Doing this is incredibly useful in a business or networking scenario if you feel a potentially important contact is slipping away. By inviting somebody else into the conversation you not only kill the silence but you also retain a connection with the contact you desire.

Smoothly Ending a Conversation

All things must come to an end, and a good conversation is one of them. Even the best conversations can end in awkward silence, but there are ways to keep that awkward parting from happening, and the best way to do this is by being aware of the situation.

Most people use body language to show that they're ready for the conversation to end. They may increase their physical distance, look around the room, or check their watch. They may also put their jacket on or look through their handbag for their keys. This doesn't mean they're bored with you or with the conversation just that they feel it should come to an end.

When this happens, wait for a short pause and offer a handshake. Look them in the eye and tell them how much you've enjoyed talking with them. You might say something like, "I really enjoyed our conversation. I'll see you later," or "It's been great talking to you, but I have to go. I'll talk to you later." Whatever you say, keep it polite and friendly, and make sure you smile. Smiling always represents a friendly gesture and it helps to show that you really mean what you say.

If you truly enjoyed the other person's company, it's perfectly acceptable to ask them to meet for coffee or lunch to continue the discussion. Offer your phone number first, and then take the other person's. Set a specific date, like next Wednesday at 11:00am, and add it to your calendar. This will ensure that your relationship won't wind up dying because neither person keeps in touch. If geographical distance makes in-person contact impossible, offer to become friends on social media and continue the conversation that way.

Closing Thoughts

Making small talk doesn't have to be scary. With a little practice, some preparation, and more practice, you will soon be able to talk to almost anyone about anything. No longer will you be bumbling through a conversation, red in the face, making others feel awkward and suffering through uncomfortable silences.

Throughout this book you've learned everything you need to be able to make effortless small talk and I want you to take a second or two to decide how you're going to leverage what you learned so you can improve your life. Are you going to expand your social circle? Are you going to set your eyes on a promotion at work? Are you looking to be less awkward in life? Are you an entrepreneur looking to network at the events you go to? Are you looking for a new romantic partner? Or, maybe it is a combination of the above.

Whatever it is you personally want set your eyes on that goal and make a conscious effort to put into practice what you've learned in this book, even a few minutes per day of practice will have a profound effect on your ability to make small talk, and therefore your life.

I strongly feel that one of the best ways to succeed in life is by putting yourself into difficult, uncomfortable situations. Getting out of your comfort zone by making small talk will help you grow as a person, meet exciting new people, develop priceless social skill and as you do this you will be amazed at the opportunities that magically seem to appear.

Enjoy the Book?

Hi,

I hope you loved the book and it helps you as much as writing it helped me.

If you enjoyed the book would you be open to leaving me a quick review on Amazon?

Reviews are crucial to the success of a book and I would love any positive feedback you have, even one sentence would be great. Writing a review would take you less than 1 minute but would be immensely beneficial to me.

So, if you're able to take a minute out of your day to leave a quick review I would be forever in your debt.

Thanks,

Andy

All rights Reserved. No part of this publication or the information in it may be quoted from or reproduced in any form by means such as printing, scanning, photocopying or otherwise without prior written permission of the copyright holder.

Disclaimer and Terms of Use: Effort has been made to ensure that the information in this book is accurate and complete, however, the author and the publisher do not warrant the accuracy of the information, text and graphics contained within the book due to the rapidly changing nature of science, research, known and unknown facts and internet. The Author and the publisher do not hold any responsibility for errors, omissions or contrary interpretation of the subject matter herein. This book is presented solely for motivational and informational purposes only.

Made in the USA
San Bernardino, CA
31 May 2019